"*Controlling Your Crazy* is your wake up call. Consider it a roadmap to avoiding stupid and taxable mistakes all in the name of love. Toni truly tells it like it is. Just a brutally honest book about what you wished you knew before getting into a relationship."

–*CREATIV Magazine*

"This book has been a long time coming. The *Controlling Your Crazy* platform has provided single women with the uncensored, raw, 'tell it like it is' advice that women NEED to hear about the dating world. The uncomfortable conversations, done in a funny and telling way, makes the content that much more relatable."

–*The Millionheiress Club, CEO*

She tells women what we *need* to hear and not what we *want* to hear. She has created an amazing platform for women to learn how to take control and to know your worth.

–*Keva J Swimwear*

# CONTROLLING YOUR
# YOUR
*Crazy*

# CONTROLLING YOUR *Crazy*

**WHILE DATING YOUR NONEXISTENT BOYFRIEND**

## Toni Douglas

Controlling Your Crazy LLC
Pembroke Pines, FL

CONTROLLING YOUR CRAZY WHILE DATING
YOUR NONEXISTENT BOYRFRIEND

This publication is designed to educate and provide general information regarding the subject matter based on the author's experiences. It is published with the understanding that neither the author nor the publisher is engaged in rendering professional counseling services and do not guarantee specific results. Each situation is different, and the advice should be tailored to particular circumstances.

CONTROLLING YOUR CRAZY WHILE DATING
YOUR NONEXISTENT BOYFRIEND
© 2020 Antonia Douglas

All rights reserved. No part of this book may be reproduced in any form or by any electronic or mechanical means including information storage and retrieval systems without permission in written form from the publisher, except by a reviewer, who may quote brief passages in a review.

Published by Controlling Your Crazy LLC
Pembroke Pines, FL

Printed in the United States
First Edition November 2020

Book Cover and Interior Design: Make Your Mark Publishing Solutions
Editing: Make Your Mark Publishing Solutions

# Contents

Acknowledgments ................................................................. ix
Preface ................................................................................ xi
Introduction ......................................................................... 1

1. My "Crazy" Experience ................................................ 11
2. Who Is the Nonexistent Boyfriend (NB)? ................... 29
3. Who Am I to the Nonexistent Boyfriend (NB)? ......... 35
4. Controlling Your Crazy While Dating Your
   Nonexistent Boyfriend ................................................ 48
5. Ditching Old Habits So You Can Control Your
   Crazy Indefinitely ........................................................ 55
6. How to Control Your Crazy After a Hurt Past ........... 68
7. Controlling Your Crazy ............................................... 75

CYCQs for Dating ............................................................... 81

# Acknowledgments

I wrote my first book!

Thank you, God. I owe my talents, creativity, and inspiration to Him. Thank you Mom and Dad for always supporting me and believing in my dreams. You two have always encouraged me to go after my goals no matter how big or small they were. Miché, thank you for being the big sister I could learn from. Because of you, I'm wiser and sassier than the woman I imagine I would be without you in my life. Josh, my baby brother, thank you for allowing me to be your go-to dating guru.

I'd like to thank all my other family members, friends, and loved ones who have supported me. *Controlling Your Crazy* is possible because of you. Your personal experiences, included with my own, provided me with the knowledge I needed to empower other women who desire a good man by their side. Marlon, my cheerleader, I love you.

## Acknowledgments

I want to thank Monique D. Mensah with Make Your Mark Publishing Solutions. Thank you for helping me self-publish my very first book. Your keep-it-real guidance was exactly what I needed to create a book women would love and need.

*Controlling Your Crazy While Dating Your Nonexistent Boyfriend* is more than just a book. It's a guide for women who want to create boundaries with the men they date and it's a guide to embrace emotional health; it is necessary for growth.

With "Crazy" Love,
*Toni*

# Preface

This book is dedicated to every woman who has had the desire to obliterate the character of a man or do something detrimental to a man because of his actions while they were dating without a commitment. This kind of woman exists everywhere.

It's only natural for a single woman who's looking for a relationship to let some of her emotional guards down when she begins dating a man. This is normal behavior because, after all, the only way for a man to really get to know a woman is for her to reveal herself in small layers, essentially letting go of any protective barriers over her heart. In addition to letting her guard down, a single woman in search of a good relationship also tends to put aside extremely harsh dating rules she's made for herself in an attempt to get to know the man she's interested in.

These dating rules could relate to sex, being willing to

try new things, or simply trusting a man again despite her past experiences. Once she bends her rules and time passes, her feelings develop in all the bliss of sappy dating—you know, late-night phone conversations, cute text messages, and fun dates with the man she's been dating and willing to get to know.

The downside to situations like the one mentioned is that, in doing this, the single woman becomes susceptible to undefined terms and somewhat counts on the emotional comfort of a man she's not officially committed to. Undefined terms become "a thing," because, let's face it, it's *just* that: undefined. No one is calling the other one "boyfriend/girlfriend," and this is where dating issues evolve. It is necessary to understand that if you are a single woman going through a stage of dating vulnerability in which you trust the man you're casually seeing, your heart becomes inadvertently entangled in a situation that shouldn't require your full emotional attention; however, it does.

Now that we're here, let's begin the breakdown of where things could possibly go wrong. There's a common denominator that seems to come up when a single woman devotes her time and thoughts to a man she's only beginning to know and learn. She becomes attached to the idea that the man she's going out to eat with and talks on the phone with is somehow *her man*. A single woman like this invests a lot of time thinking of what things *could* be with said man, rather than taking her situation for what it is: a feel-good friendship.

While some men on the dating scene play a tremendous role in making the women they date feel as though they are the only one they're seeing, these same women fall victim to their own feelings. First and foremost, a single woman is *not* to blame for having feelings and wanting to honor what a man tells her. She should not be made to feel guilty for "feeling." Single women only fall victim to their feelings when they assume single men are dating one woman exclusively, that woman being her. Therefore, it is important for single women to lean on factors other than their feelings, so they do not end up getting hurt.

For example, a single woman should date around. She should not hone in on one man in the early stages of dating. "Dating around" means giving yourself options while you're deciding who you'd like to spend a significant amount of time with. It also means being able to lay out the pros and cons of each man you entertain, so as not to wind up getting deep feelings involved for the potentially "wrong" person. Unfortunately, the phrase "dating around" sometimes carries negative connotations; however, it's the exact opposite when it comes to reserving feelings and sentimental emotions. In a nutshell, seeing more than one man at a time relieves emotional tension, (*i.e.,* removes the idea of thinking about one man all the time) and allows *any* woman to weigh her options so she does not make hasty decisions.

Another issue that seems to be universal for single women is the notion that, at some point while dating, they will come across men who are deliberately distant toward them and will not know how to react. Casually dating a man who suddenly becomes distant or emotionally disconnected is not a good feeling; it usually leaves a single woman feeling confused or possibly undesirable. However, understanding that this will occur at least once while dating, and knowing that the men who tend to do this lack communication skills, will change the dating game completely. I'll address some of the reasons this may have happened to you or *will* happen to you while you're dating. I will also explain the appropriate way to respond to his emotional absence if/when it occurs.

The first thing to know is that not all men will want the same things as you after they get to know you or have hung out with you. For example, you may meet a man and he discovers after a very short while that you're not a woman who only wants to date for sexual pleasure; you want something serious. He wants a woman to have sexual fun with, and you're not the woman who's willing to do that. As a result, he'll become disconnected by possibly cutting of communication, not coming around, or making excuses for inexplainable behaviors. While this may not feel good to you, going into the dating scene knowing this could happen and how to address it is key.

You may even meet and begin to casually date a man who you've built a connection with. Although you're not in a relationship with him, you've developed some feelings toward him and thought he did the same toward you. Out of the blue, he may become emotionally detached from you because he doesn't want to lead you on and make you believe your casual dating can turn into something exclusive. Again, it's not the best feeling in the world, but because of your preparedness and knowledge on how to react in this type of situation, your feelings can be spared when it's time to move on.

While the reasons for why men pull away vary, the bottom line is you have to be aware that this is an unfortunate occurrence in dating today and understand that responding to it correctly will bring on a healthy emotional state for you. So, how should you respond when this occurs?

Most times, the man you meet will let you know what he's looking for in the long run with dating. If he doesn't blatantly express this, his actions will do the talking for him (in both positive and negative occurrences). He will express his dating desires with you in a casual phone conversation, through a text conversation, or even on a date. Be aware that this doesn't mean a man can't be lying about his desires, but for the most part, he'll always tell you. After you've revealed what you're looking for while dating or even revealed parts of you that come through naturally while you're casually dating, there will be an outcome; he will either want to remain connected with you, or he will want to disconnect.

If the man you're casually dating decides to suddenly withdraw or disconnect from you, you should respond in a way that reveals your true feelings without being sappy, apologetic, or weak. This doesn't mean you respond in a way that promotes anger or rage, rather it means you're truthful to him about what you felt and what you thought, making sure your emotions directly align to what has transpired over time. For example, if you've been going out on dates and talking to a man for about six weeks, it's pretty safe to say you're getting comfortable with him and your current dating situation. If that man decides to pull away for whatever reason, it is your job to respond to what he did by letting him know how you feel about his withdrawal (without cursing, threats, or ultimatums) and *why* you feel the way you do based on the things he may have overtly said or done.

This reaction is not one to convince him to stick around *or* force him to give his "why." Because you are single and should be confident in who you are, it is never your job to figure out why he has become disconnected. If he cannot communicate that to you on his own free will, you should accept that while making sure your thoughts and feelings toward him are clear. If he didn't value your presence, don't force him to; another man will.

It's important you don't ignore what a man says regarding his desires in dating and become blinded by the fantasy of wanting to have a man. What I mean by that is don't hear what you want to hear from him and convince yourself that he'll seek interest in your desires or change his mind about how he feels or what he wants out of dating. You should listen intently to the things he says, as he should listen intently to the things you say. Hear his truth, take it in, and make the decision to either go along with it or not. Worrying about whether the two of you will be in a relationship should come much later.

Despite all the dos and don'ts, there is a ton of good news behind it all. The reality of dating today is that women *always* have control in the situation. Women oversee what information they give *and* what information they take away from men the moment they meet them. What you'll discover throughout this book, and what you should have discovered already while dating, is that men say and do a lot of things that affect the women they date, be it positive or negative. Again, what a man says and does is not in your control. What *is* in your control is the way you react in response to their behaviors. Having control while dating and knowing you have control is a must. You have control because *you* are in charge of your emotions, because there are no strings attached when you meet a man, and because there are no promises to keep or mandates to meet. You're able to create your own outcomes, even if a man does something negative or misleading.

No matter what a man does or says while you're casually dating him (ruling out abusive behaviors, of course), you never want to lose control. Losing control creates tension and creating tension will cause you to react erratically or worse, angrily. Reactions like those ruin your chances of being emotionally at rest. It can affect your day-to-day living, and it can certainly affect how you date and respond to men in the future. No woman should want an unhealthy dating life, nor should they want to bring on an unhealthy expression of their emotions. Knowing you're in control of your reactions and maintaining your control puts you in the position to be wise in how you'll channel your emotions, and that often makes for positive outcomes.

One way you can maintain control while casually dating is to not give the man you're getting to know *all* your free time and mental energy. If you're already thinking, *Well, how will I get to know him?* or *How will I know if he's the right man for me?* you need to remember that his role is to actively pursue you while you simply maintain your emotional energy. Not devoting all your free time and mental energy into a man you're casually dating is essential because, let's be real, it is not guaranteed that your dating situation will manifest into something greater. This is not to deter you from the possibility of a casual dating situation evolving into something great, but it's about understanding that not pouring all of yourself into the relationship from the very beginning will help you control your feelings and how you respond to that man's behavior down the line.

You must understand that men are not obligated to devote their all to women they're getting to know or are beginning to date casually. I don't care what a single man preaches or what he does in an effort to court a woman. A man should not be held to *any* emotional obligation from a woman he's not committed to; and the same goes for a woman who's not committed to a man. No man should hold her to an emotional standard. All of the information in this book will emphasize the notion that if there is no shared title and/or commitment between a single woman and a single man, there should be no demands made. Demands could include making it a requirement to get into a relationship by a specific time or even the obligation for a man to provide certain things (monetary, emotional, physical) according to your standards.

To avoid having to make these demands, men and women should always communicate their desires when dating. Honesty and openness should be at the forefront of initial conversations, and sincere actions should follow. This concept must be understood. Not being honest about what you want, even in a causal relationship, could lead single women, like you, into feeling let down by the men they *think* they have a title with but really don't. Your feelings could get overshadowed by "what it should be" rather than "what it is." Being an open book can avoid a lot of confusion later, and it could dismiss uncertainties that come with hidden feelings.

The information in this book should not be viewed as "rules" on how to date single men. Rather, it should be viewed as a guide that can help you maintain a mental and emotional space that allows you to feel, but not in a way that'll compromise your temperament or normal behavior. This is a book based on some of my beliefs and experiences, views of other women and *their* experiences, and a whole bunch of hypotheticals and truths in between. Now that that's out of the way, I'd like to be very clear on a few things.

First, who you decide to date is entirely up to you. Where you decide to go on dates, how you choose to communicate with a man you're beginning to date, and what you choose to believe from a man you're getting to know is also completely up to you. Deciding when to become intimate or what activities to engage in with the men you're casually dating is a personal decision that has nothing to do with what this book discusses. The content you'll unfold in this book is all about how to react while dating a man with whom you have no commitment to.

If there happens to be a mutual understanding (a title, exclusivity) between you and a man you're dating, then the rules of dating become altered a bit. If you and a potential suitor eventually get serious, you and that man are agreeing to invest time and space in one another. If there is not an agreed upon title or commitment, there shouldn't be an assumption as to what *should* happen, what you believe he *should* be doing, and how he *should* devote one hundred percent of his time and energy into you. (Remember, you cannot control his behaviors or emotions, only yours.) Thinking this way is not fair to him or you, and more importantly, there is the potential for repercussions (broken hearts) when these dating assumptions occur.

...

With all this newfound knowledge, we'll briefly delve into the most important aspect of this book and the word that seems to plague single women: crazy. While men *are* guilty of throwing the term "crazy" around while dating women, I prefer to hold on to it for the sake of understanding what women need to know. I am in no way justifying the term, nor am I excusing the men who use it as a weapon to hurt, humiliate, or degrade a woman. I am, however, using the term to help single women in their quest to develop healthy friendships with the men they casually date while continuing to control their emotions, even if the outcome of the relationship doesn't turn out the way they imagined it would.

When I use the term "crazy" in relation to dating, I am not emphasizing the obvious connotations that are centered around it. These connotations usually refer to behaviors that could have very harsh consequences, sometimes involving the law. Instead, I use the term to emphasize emotional reactions that are expressed when a woman is dating a man she likes but, for some reason, is not feeling obliged by the way he's dating or liking *her*.

I've already pointed out that I've been privy to other women's experiences and views on dating. Through that, I have made a discovery. Many single women naturally take on the attitude that somehow, they're owed a man's time and emotions once the two of them get past a certain level (whatever the woman dictates without the man's knowledge). For example, because a single woman may be happy with the man she's met and she's content with what he brings to the table and how he's treating her, she assumes the man feels emotionally connected to her without him actually saying it. However, he should *always* say it; it shouldn't be a secret.

With that knowing, I bring in the term "crazy" to show that it is unreasonable to believe that a man who a woman is beginning to know should feel the exact way she does just because things "feel good" to her. Sure, humans connect in a way that is sometimes unspoken, but assuming a person feels the same way you do about them without them acknowledging it can cause a lot of confusion.

Again, the idea of being "crazy" is not the craziness that should have you in a psychiatric ward or one that could necessarily have you behind bars. You'll learn that this form of crazy is the one that stresses you the *hell* out when you act on emotional impulse and aren't able to maintain the control you should have with a man you're not in a relationship with.

Acting on emotional impulse rather than slow, rational thinking could have you doing or saying things that could lead you to feel embarrassed, regretful of any silly actions, and like you want to lash out. You could even be called "crazy" by the man you imagined future dates with or shared a title with. Whether a man *thinks* he has reasons for referring to you as "crazy" is up to him; you're not bound by his title. However, always keep in mind that it is your goal to exit the friendship with him knowing that all of your actions while dating him were mature and justified and your ability to move on and maintain your peace was never compromised. This doesn't dismiss any wrongdoings on his part, but it holds you accountable for how you respond to any situation you face while casually dating him.

In a nutshell, by the end of this book, you'll be able to decipher between what is and what isn't while you're casually dating a man. You'll also be able to clearly define what is "crazy" versus what is natural while dating a man you are not committed to. I'll present common unfavorable scenarios with steps you can take to avoid confusion. This book will help you control the energy you give and receive while dating a man who really isn't yours. Page by page, you'll grasp the concept of what it means to control your "crazy" while you're dating. You'll understand the importance of holding back irrational emotions, even when the man you're seeing does something absurd, acts immaturely, or disrespects you, and ultimately, you'll learn to control the urge to immediately react and act out.

# Introduction

Now that we're here, things may get a bit fuzzy, but your understanding will become clearer as you move along through this book. I'm only using the term "fuzzy" because you may not want to adjust to the word "crazy" just yet. However, understand that the word "crazy" is being used to assist you while you date more than it is being used to criticize or condemn you for your feelings.

See, acting crazily isn't always what many men or women have labeled it to be. Because the definition in this case is based on women's emotional responses to men's actions, "crazy" can't be assigned to one unusual behavior. Reducing "crazy" to one definition is like trying to reduce the definition of being smart. For example, there are so many particulars when trying to determine if one is "smart." It's impossible to simply have one concrete definition or understanding of what being smart is. The same concept applies to being crazy. While "crazy" can take on several meanings, there are indicators I use to help identify your craziness while casually dating.

The first thing to understand is that there's a spectrum of craziness. For example, you could be the "bat-swinging, toss bleach on your clothing" crazy, or you could simply be the girl who won't stay off his social media page, lurking for clues surrounding his dating life. Either way you slice it, both types of behaviors result in crazy acting and/or thinking. I know accepting a title such as "crazy" is a hard pill to swallow. It's mainly difficult because many single women have been hurt or let down by the men they have chosen to date at some point in their lives. More importantly, men have been guilty of tossing the term around when it's unwarranted. However, accepting the term head on and acknowledging when you've exhibited actions in situations that weren't worth your emotional energy is the start to controlling your crazy.

By my own definition, controlling your crazy while dating your Nonexistent Boyfriend is always about being emotionally responsible with your feelings. "Controlling your crazy" doesn't mean you're not allowed to cry, express sappy emotions, mope, whine, or yell. Instead, it means, if you can help it, you should *never* cry, express sappy emotions, mope, whine, or yell to/at a man you're casually dating for *any* reason. Sure, you should communicate how you feel when you're dating someone; it's the mature and right thing to do to get your points and feelings across. But it is critical to recognize that the man you're beginning to date should not be subject to receiving your emotional breakdowns or tangents because you believe it comes with the territory of dating you.

Remember, when you're beginning to date a man, he is not someone you should become emotionally attached to simply because it's difficult to attach yourself to someone emotionally when you don't have enough knowledge of who they are and what significance they'll have in your life yet. Again, it's not to say you shouldn't express certain emotions, but the wrong emotions you choose to express to a man you're beginning to date are the defining factors that normalize your unwise behaviors or make them crazy.

Another factor to consider is that "controlling your crazy" means to never step out of your emotional comfort zone. When you control your crazy in this way, you can avoid getting let down or feeling silly for forcefully putting yourself out there when the man you like hasn't done the same. For example, when you were a little girl and you *really* liked a boy in your class, you'd get emotional (whether internally or externally) when the boy didn't like you the way you liked him. Once you learned this boy wasn't on the same page as you, your first reaction was to probably respond with whatever behavior came to mind. This behavior could have resulted in you writing him an inquiring note, having a friend convince him you were special, or even subtly walking past him in hopes that he'll muster up the courage to be your special playmate. You put yourself in a position to potentially get let down because the little boy you had the hots for didn't reciprocate your same feelings and you didn't give him a chance to.

When newly dating a man, you don't want to be that little girl. You want to avoid stepping out of your emotional comfort zone by controlling your crazy. When you like a man, create some time to determine if he feels the same way. Throwing it all on the table by inquiring how he feels early on, having other people speak to him on your behalf, or making yourself overly present can show a lack of emotional control. Instead, be the great woman you are by letting the man you like or are casually dating come to his own realization. Your dating process will go smoother, and you'll be able to hold back premature actions that would otherwise not work in your favor if he is not interested in you *that* way.

While many women, myself included, hate to admit it, we've all engaged in a manner that was uncharacteristically normal for us. That is to say, we behaved in a manner that isn't who we are or who we want to be when a man we date does something unusual, suspicious, or insensitive. You see, "crazy" doesn't have to be some wild, obnoxious action. Again, it's a kind of crazy that's based on emotions, so oftentimes, going crazy could be subtle. Going crazy simply means you've lost some control over your feelings, and it puts the man you like in a position to determine his fate with you. Whether or not he's aware of his newfound position, it'll feel as though he calls the shots on where the two of you stand because you've surrendered a portion of your emotions into his hands. This is *not* to say that you have no control over yourself or your feelings; rather, it's to argue that if you've fallen victim to going crazy, it's because you were emotionally overwhelmed and did what it took to feel better.

I'll be the first to admit that men say and do a lot of things that can infuriate, confuse, betray, or even annoy the crap out of women while they're casually dating them. However, women have no control over men's behaviors, so it's something that must be understood but dealt with accordingly.

The beauty about us women is that we have amazing intuitive power. Our intuition and insight into things make us aware of what's happening around us before it even happens! Because we have this ability, we must use it when we're dating. Oftentimes, we "go crazy" or have gone crazy for a man we were casually dating because we looked passed our intuition, hoping for the best outcome. We *knew* something didn't feel right or we *knew* something didn't sound believable, but we rolled with the punches anyway until, eventually, we let our emotions get the best of us.

The inability to control your crazy almost feels like the man you're casually dating has something over you. Again, even if he's not aware of it, it's present because of how you respond to situations and let certain emotions consume you. The silver lining in all of this is that once you understand how to control your crazy and establish what "going crazy" is, you'll develop an emotional skill that will stop unnecessary emotions in their tracks while processing how to be in charge of what you relay and project to the man you have no commitment to.

Now that you've been introduced to the phrase "controlling your crazy" and understand that "going crazy" doesn't mean what you thought it did, I've provided a list of common actions that can be categorized as "going crazy." These actions are often performed by single women who are casually dating a man they like, and these women are sometimes unaware that they're even giving into their emotions and losing control of their feelings and/or reactions.

The following acts are considered "crazy" when casually dating a man:

- Checking/going through his phone when he's not aware
- Calling him and hanging up to determine his availability
- Having a friend act like an interested suitor to test his "commitment" to your situation (most likely via social media)
- Creating fake social media pages to spy on him
- Driving by his job/house unannounced to see if he's there or if someone else (i.e., a woman) is there
- Calling/texting him repeatedly after failed attempts of contact
- Disguising/hiding your phone number in hopes that he'll answer the phone when you call
- Following other women on social media who may appear to have interest in him
- Using tears/harsh emotions to give him unnecessary guilt trips or to exaggerate normal feelings
- Lying about going out with other men/friends to make him jealous
- Hacking into his cell phone records and/or email
- Befriending his ex-girlfriend to learn more about him (usually via online)
- Damaging his property (i.e., car, phone, house, personal belongings)

- Threatening to physically harm him
- Calling his job for arbitrary reasons without his consent
- Attempting to harm yourself to make him worry about you
- Reaching out to his family/friends to locate him
- Persuading him to take you out on dates
- Teasing him with sexual innuendos to gauge how much he likes you
- Demanding to meet his parents/family members
- Repeatedly inquiring about where you and he stand very early on (in a case where he honestly conveyed his feelings already)
- Allowing him to use you for monetary gifts, items, or sex in hopes of a commitment

While this list could extend throughout the entire book, it provides you with common behaviors that exhibit a "crazy" side. While casually dating a man, a woman should always try to avoid engaging in the actions mentioned. What she should do instead is set strong boundaries for herself. She could also make better choices in the men she chooses to date by acknowledging her intuition while recognizing and avoiding red flags. More importantly, a woman should have enough discipline to walk away from a situation that makes her physically or emotionally uncomfortable. These are all major factors in controlling your crazy.

Remember, it is never about keeping quiet to please the man you like or are beginning to date. It's more about being aware of your feelings, addressing them appropriately, and knowing how to gracefully run for the door if things don't pan out as you imagined.

# Chapter One

## MY "CRAZY" EXPERIENCE

Before delving into who the "Nonexistent Boyfriend" is and what the entire concept means, there is one important part of my life I think should be shared. I'm sharing this to show you that no matter who you are or what you've been through as a single woman, you can control the inner emotions that make you want to act up when you don't need to. The part of my life that I'm referring to was a time when my "crazy" wasn't controlled. I let my emotions get the best of me, and I acted in a way that belittled who I really was. I was a confident, smart, and kind young woman, but I didn't show those sides of me when I was put into a situation where my emotions and feelings were compromised.

I remember my "crazy" moment like it was yesterday.

Here I am today, almost twenty years removed from the incident, but my crazy moment is as clear as day in my memory. I never knew "crazy" was in me until it became me, and that's exactly where my story begins.

I was a young woman in college beginning to enter a new phase in my life: my twenties. Life was pretty good then. I had no real worries other than making sure I didn't party too long with friends in time to wake up for college classes the next day. Basically, I was midway through my college career, and I was having, what I thought, was the time of my life with my closest friends and family.

> **I was a confident, smart, and kind young woman, but I didn't show those sides of me when I was put into a situation where my emotions and feelings were compromised.**

During these worry-free times, I was independently in charge of my every move, and I felt liberated enough to make my own choices when it came to dating. Although my parents never restricted me from dating in my late teens, I still had no one to tell me who I should and shouldn't date, and I prided myself on making grown-up decisions with my love life. Although my first love came into my life late in my college career, I had the notion that I knew *all* the basic rules when it came to relationships; boy, was I wrong. I thought I knew more than I really did about dating because

I was always the friend who offered objective advice to my girlfriends, and I was also the friend who knew how to classily brush things off my shoulders with guys, even when they were obnoxious or appeared heartless toward me. I developed somewhat of a hardened heart because of the tricks and schemes I knew young men liked to play, and I carried that hardened heart with me as I began my phase of collegiate dating.

I went to Florida State University, one the biggest universities in Florida, and I had some of the best friends there. While in school, my social life consisted of campus hangouts, careless shopping, and late-night eating after weekend partying. While it's safe to say my social life was appealing, my love life wasn't so great at one point.

At the age of twenty, I had just gotten out of a very long friendship and relationship with a high school sweetheart who later turned into a college love. Now, for me, this was no ordinary relationship (or what I *thought* was ordinary); he was someone I had liked since the age of fourteen! Our first middle school encounter was the first time I had truly felt that "thing" most girls, and even women, talk about when first meeting a guy. For the sake of privacy, I'll refer to him as "Jason."

Jason was one of the cuter guys I had dated in my middle school years, or so I thought. And like me, he loved to sport the latest clothing trends and brag about his eye for fashion. Although Jason and I were young, we developed an intense fixation for each other. We never missed the opportunity to share love notes, and we loved the idea of having phone conversations before our parents would come home to intercept the phone line. Although our meaningless middle school relationship never ran its proper course, Jason and I remained very good friends and flirting buddies.

Luckily for me, I transitioned from middle school and went to the same high school as him, and there, we discovered our infatuation for each other was still present. We never engaged in a full-on relationship during the first part of high school, but all of that changed once we got older. As we neared the end of our senior year, Jason and I decided to give a *real* relationship a try. I was eighteen years old and thought I was mature enough to seriously date Jason. By the time I graduated high school and entered college, I was basking in true love and everything it had to offer. I had developed the kind of feelings for Jason that made it *impossible* to think of being in love with anyone else—literally, no one. It was my first real experience with the variety of feelings and emotions women endure in their love life. There were plenty of hugs and kisses, fun dates, laughter, endless photos, and intimacy.

While love is indeed a beautiful part of our existence, I

was naïve to how love in relationships *should* be. Meaning, I didn't know love was supposed to be two-sided and that both parties should feel the same way about each other for the relationship to flourish. Unfortunately for me at that time, Jason and I broke up after a two-year stint. While I would love to say the breakup was mutual, Jason decided to go his own way after we had one too many disagreements on how we felt about each other. I wasn't sure if I wanted to date other people, and Jason had already began dating someone else, unbeknownst to me.

After getting out of this friendship that had lasted nearly seven years, and a relationship that lasted for two of those years, I didn't know where my love life left me. I didn't know who else could capture my heart and make me comfortable enough to love so immensely. Sure, I moved on and began dating and meeting new people after Jason and I split, but I was in a small college town, cycling through the young men all the other college women had already dealt with at some point. While I *should* have been phasing out of love with Jason based on how we ended and the fact that we both moved on, my emotions for him kept yo-yoing, making it impossible for me to "let go." A big part of my uncertainty was due to Jason leading me to believe there'd be hope for us in the future. Not to be outdone, Jason and I still talked daily and were routinely intimate; this made my love life very difficult. One fact remained, however: Jason and I were not in a committed relationship, and there was no established exclusivity. We were both irresponsibly rolling with the punches.

On one particular night, I had a weird, tingly mental feeling. It was the feeling most women get when they suspect the guy they like is up to no good or is trying to play emotional games. I felt like Jason had been lying to me about his whereabouts during a weekend he spent out of town. His behavior seemed abnormal because I was accustomed to talking to him every day and night, and now, I wasn't. Every attempt I made to call and speak with him over the phone quickly turned into an "I'll call you right back!" That, too, was strange. What could be making Jason so busy?

I thought Jason *owed* it to me to tell me the truth about where he really went for the weekend, and I also thought he was obligated to tell me who he was with! Silly me. The night he returned from his weekend out of town, I had the sudden urge to get out of bed and move on reactionary emotions and feelings. I had the right to feel the way I felt, but I never stopped to ponder the "what ifs" or any forms of proper communication with him. I simply reacted.

I jumped out of bed and covered my hair with an overused scarf. I also put on pajamas that were way too hot for the time of year, so I looked ridiculous, to say the least.

Without much thinking, I picked up the phone and immediately called one of my girlfriends. I called her to accompany me on a journey I had not anticipated or fully thought out. I started our phone conversation by telling her to listen, and she did. When I told my friend I wanted her to come with me to go to Jason's house unannounced, she never stopped me in my tracks nor warned me of what could go wrong. Because of that, I convinced myself I was about to do the right thing. I alerted my friend that if I did anything that night that was out of my character or made me look foolish, she should write it off as me just being "a girl."

I got in my car, left my house, and took pleasure in knowing that no one could stop me. I headed to my girlfriend's house, and like clockwork, she was ready and waiting for me at her front door. She got in my car and took the two-mile drive with me in what I remember to be dead silence. If my friend spoke to me or asked me any questions during our car ride, I wouldn't have known because my brain was clouded with scenarios I would potentially encounter.

I made it to Jason's apartment complex in what seemed like thirty seconds. Although I had been in his complex several times before, it looked strangely different that night. Left turns didn't seem right, and corners became straight roads as I drove in what seemed like a daze. My actions that night were clearly unexpected, but I relished in the fact that

I finally had the upper hand after feeling dismissed for an entire weekend. After taking my usual route into his complex, I saw Jason's car in its assigned spot. Usually, I'd blush in anticipation before darting up the stairs to see him. This time, I didn't know what to make of the car I was so used to seeing. I realized then that me failing to plan a proper meet-up would result in an absolute disaster; I was literally stuck with no plan.

The dew in the air that night produced moisture on Jason's car windows. At first, I wanted to jump out of my car and write the words "Fuck you" on his window. That plan was quickly dismissed because my common sense assured me those words would fade away the moment I drove off. Even though I couldn't write the words I was thinking, those same words ignited something inside of me. I was confused, anxious, and jittery all at once. I was no longer sure what I was doing in Jason's complex. My heart was leading me in one direction, while my brain was telling me to press the gas and keep driving around the complex; I followed suit.

Something happened. Something really bad happened at this point. As I cruised around the complex, my feelings of anxiety suddenly turned into anger. I noticed another car parked amongst the cars in the apartment complex. It looked familiar. It was a car I knew all too well because I had seen my ex-boyfriend around this car quite often. It was another young lady's car, a young lady my ex-boyfriend had denied ever being with. My instincts knew differently, and that night proved it. This young lady didn't live in Jason's complex, and she and Jason had no family ties. I could only think of the next logical question, *Why the fuck is she here?!*

It was almost two in the morning the night I found myself driving around my ex's complex. I had previously convinced myself that I hadn't driven to his neighborhood in vein, so before the sun came up, I immediately confirmed a plan and knew what had to be done.

I parked my car haphazardly.

"Wait for me," I said to my friend, as I reached for the car's door handle.

I walked to the building Jason lived in, and I marched up to the second floor. My mind was in such a blur that night. To be honest, I have no memory of even wearing shoes; I can laugh about it *now*. After walking up two flights of stairs, I approached Jason's apartment door and froze. I stood in one spot, staring at his door as though it had deceived me for letting me in so many times. I knocked on the door of his apartment once and waited. There was a silence in the neighborhood that seemed to engulf me. It could've been my nervousness, my anger, or maybe I simply drowned out any noise that had existed. I knocked on the door a second time with the violence of a landlord collecting his late rent.

I waited again in silence and watched as an onlooker walked past me to his own apartment door. I literally felt like I was open to any and *everything* at this point because, after all, I was knocking on Jason's door in the middle of the night with hot PJs on and an unkempt appearance.

Jason opened his door, despite my bullyish knock; I was completely stunned. I expected him to *not* open the door because of the intensity behind my knock *and* because it was so late into the night. I didn't imagine he'd still be awake or would even want to address someone knocking so hard. I never rehearsed what I would say that night, and I certainly never expected Jason to put me in this predicament. This was all his fault. Jason made me do this. I relinquished taking any responsibility in my current situation because I didn't want to believe I could simply walk away from him any time I wanted to.

Once his door reluctantly opened, I did the first thing that came to mind. I didn't hesitate, and I tried to shove past Jason like an Oakland Raider diving in for a last-minute touchdown. I nudged, and I pushed, and I yelled. My lousy football tackle attempt couldn't get past his stance, so I did the next best thing I could think of: I grabbed him by his shirt collar and held on for dear life. His resistance to let me in suddenly told me someone else was inside. It was almost as if I felt a certain energy coming from his front door. I let that feeling lead me in the wrong direction, and I began yelling things to him, like "Liar!" "Devil!" "Bastard!" and "I'm pregnant!" (Yes, I went there. I went there because it was very possible I could've been.)

I yelled and said anything that sounded believable. I went to great lengths to coerce him into explaining why he had been lying to me about his intentions when it came to us and about possibly being involved with someone else. I questioned him and drilled him within two short minutes. Jason had no answer for me other than, "You're crazy!" Go figure. He was right. I was acting crazy over a situation I *thought* I had no control over. I had all the control in the world, but I allowed my emotions to talk me out of properly communicating with him, walking away from our noncommittal situation, and moving on for good.

Two minutes of shouting from me quickly turned into ten minutes of chaos, and after that, I lost track of time. I forced Jason to walk down to the bottom of his apartment building's stairs. I held onto his shirt collar as we walked down the steps in synchronicity, stair by stair. During my moment of madness, I screamed unforgettable obscenities. Honestly, I don't even remember the words I said; I just knew they were all bad, but it felt right in that moment.

When we hit that bottom step, I looked deeply into Jason's eyes. I thought to myself, *This is the young boy I had eyes for since the eighth grade. He became one of the closest people in my life, and here he is lying to me. He was supposed to love me and never betray me, no matter what. This is the young man who had convinced me that saving myself for marriage was too long of a wait because he could offer something special before then. Here he is, finally pushing me out of his life.*

Collar grabbing graduated to pajama pant grabbing (*yes, I went there, too*), and I had lost complete control of myself. I lost the morals I was raised with and the pride to never make a spectacle in public. I never threw any fists at Jason, nor did I do anything worth having someone call the police on me, but I had stepped outside of my realm. At the end of a mediocre tussle and unanswered questions, Jason had had enough with my antics.

He raised his closed fist high into the air and brought it down with the pressure of a testosterone-filled man. That pressure landed on top of my shaking hand in an effort to make me let go of his pajama pants. *Shit!* It hurt. By now, the neighbors had come out of their quiet apartments to entertain the ruckus that had ensued in the complex. Like typical teenagers and young adults, their minds needed gossip-worthy stories to relay to friends. Thank God the technology of smartphones and social media platforms hadn't reared its head yet; I was saved by the early 2000s, whose years were not advanced enough to capture what was happening with foolish college women in love.

Something happened after he pounded my hand. A new and different emotion came over me, while some weird epiphany simultaneously hit me. In one split second, I let go of his pajama bottoms, and I looked at him. He stared back at me like a confused puppy. Even *he* couldn't believe I was acting in a way he had never imagined. It felt like I exhaled the kind of breath you'd only see in cold weather, only it was hot all around me. I walked away from Jason and returned to my car. I walked past onlookers, parked cars, and what felt like peeping eyes from second-story windows.

I got to my car, and I sat inside. Of course, my friend, who had been waiting on me, immediately asked me what happened. She hadn't heard a word of what transpired between Jason and me, and I wasn't prepared to tell her yet. Imagine that. My debacle and heart-wrenching episode was no more than one hundred feet away from my car, and my friend was oblivious to the tug-of-war contest between me and Jason's clothes. I began driving away from the parking spot I had originally sped into. I had every intention of speeding away like a race car driver. Instead, I reversed slowly, used my mirrors as cautionary measures, and kept my head straight. On my way out of the complex, I caught a glimpse of the young lady who I suspected was inside of Jason's apartment. She walked away from his apartment building toward her car, visibly pissed; it was the same walk I endured moments earlier. That walk was like traveling down an invisible hallway with a "Walk of Shame" sign hanging above my head.

I drove my girlfriend back to her house while briefly telling her the story she never got to witness. Then, I drove home. I took my sorry ass to bed, and I vowed, from that day forward, I would never go crazy again when it involved a man. I would never devote that much energy to someone to get nothing in return—and not just anyone, a Nonexistent Boyfriend. I performed all these antics for a man I was not committed to. Jason and I no longer shared a title with each other, and I let an intimate friendship go on way past its expiration date; I could've walked away.

I realized I was single, completely single. I had this warped way of thinking back then that because me and my ex-boyfriend were intimately involved and had shared so many things together, I was somehow able to have rights no other woman had. I didn't know that unless there was communication about relationship statuses and a clear understanding of what my future would look like with a man I was dating, I couldn't hold him accountable for *anything* he did with another woman. Morally, my ex had a responsibility to respect me and treat me as someone with feelings. Allowing him to get away with sending mixed signals or lying in my bed whenever he wanted to didn't give him the right to string me along. However, he was not my partner. He never asked me to be his girlfriend, and he didn't put in the work toward building a *real* relationship. Right there is where I had to take responsibility for how I let the situation play out.

After my "crazy" night, I learned a lot of important lessons I carry with me to this day. I learned that I am one hundred percent responsible for all of my actions. What I decide to believe, accept, and tolerate from a man I have no commitment with is completely up to me and no one else. I cannot expect someone to care for me the way I care for them unless we exchange marital vows or make an honest commitment to one another that involves a mutual title and mutual respect for one another's emotions. I also learned what it feels like to care for someone, or even like someone, I'm not in a relationship with. More importantly, I know how it feels to be led on by someone who doesn't even seem like they care.

What I took away most from my experience back then was that my ex turned into my Nonexistent Boyfriend, meaning he was no different than any other guy I met and was casually dating. Sure, we had a past, but our past shouldn't have had any bearing on our current situation; we were no longer together. My experience showed me I was at fault for believing Jason would eventually come around and we would somehow magically get back together, even though we weren't investing quality time into one another. Again, Jason should take ownership in what transpired after he and I broke up. What he doesn't have to do is take responsibility for my actions the night I acted belligerently.

Now that my past with Jason is behind me and I experienced my own crazy dating story, I now know that my ex-boyfriend was nonexistent the entire time I was being casually intimate with him. My ex-boyfriend was physically there but was completely emotionally absent from my life. For me, this meant he was someone I expected to be my partner, even though he wasn't. Although he was present in the flesh, his emotions toward me and our potential relationship were absent. Jason and I were friends, but that was the problem for me. I wanted us to be more than friends, and I know now that he didn't want more from me. I let a few words of seduction, several nights of sex, and memories from our past lure me from reality. I thought he was in control of the situation with us, and I thought I could convince him to change the way he felt about me.

All along, I had complete control of every step I took in my love life with Jason. I had the ability to make decisions and steer my love life in a way that didn't prioritize what

I thought could come out of something Jason never mentioned; I've learned a lot since then.

So, there it is, a point in my life where I couldn't "control my crazy." I had a difficult time channeling my feelings, and I didn't know how to prevent myself from investing my all into a causal relationship. I chose one night to behave irrationally, and my feelings got the best of me. There were several ways I could've dealt with the situation. I could have easily had a phone conversation with Jason, or I could've taken it a step further and sat with him face-to-face. This would have allowed me to express how his actions or comments made me feel.

I understand I didn't have the right to show up to his apartment unannounced, and I didn't have the right to touch him violently; things could've gotten crazier than what they did. I *did* have the right to tell him how I felt but not in the way I chose. I believe I was unable to speak from a place of authenticity with my ex-boyfriend because I relinquished my control. I left it up to him to decide our fate, and I wasn't up front about my feelings after we broke up. Sure, I told him I loved him, but I didn't express what I desired and what I wanted out of casually dating him. Be it as it may, because of my experience *then*, I'm free from irresponsibly acting out *now*. I know the importance of being heard without having to act or think crazily. I also know how essential it is for a man to be honest and for me to create an outcome that is best for me and my feelings when he's not.

The reason I've shared my experience is to help *all* single women, particularly those who have a hard time expressing their emotions or those who are not aware of the control they possess while dating. I'm also sharing my experience to help you understand that negative occurrences can happen while dating. However, you can be deliberate in what you think and how you react so you don't respond in ways that appear careless or powerless to the men you're dating.

# Chapter Two

## WHO IS THE NONEXISTENT BOYFRIEND (NB)?

While many of us would like to believe that the term "nonexistent" only refers to something that is not tangible or isn't there, this expression will take on a whole new meaning in this book. I will explain how something that is nonexistent can be as noticeable as the fact that you're completely single. I will also explain how the term can reshape and redefine how you look at the men you date.

For starters, you are here to understand what role a man plays in your life from the moment you meet him. He plays the role of someone who has no emotional connection to you because he doesn't know you. This doesn't mean developing an emotional connection with him is impossible; rather, you shouldn't be concerned with it while casually dating him. You two are simply getting to know each other.

Some single women have a hard time letting their all-knowing intuition and discernment for bullshit take a front seat in their encounters with men. Instead, some single women let their delicate side, their innate emotional side, lead the way. A portion of dating mishaps occur because some single women resist being someone who knows exactly what she wants and lets the part of herself that's willing to take a chance on a "maybe" lead the way.

When you lead with your emotions this way, it's hard to decipher between what's substantial and what has no substance at all. Something substantial would be a man telling the woman he's casually dating that he wants to take things to the next level and actively participating in making it happen. A situation without substance would be a man who is not living up to his words or a man who vehemently states he never wanted a relationship to begin with. Just because you meet men, talk to them, spend casual time with them, or exchange interesting and engaging dialogue with them, it

> *A portion of dating mishaps occur because some single women resist being someone who knows exactly what she wants and lets the part of herself that's willing to take a chance on a "maybe" lead the way.*

doesn't mean they're somehow committed to you beyond the surface. Any man, from day one, is nonexistent. This nonexistent man is the man who is physically attainable but serves no purpose emotionally because he hasn't committed to a relationship with you nor has he promised himself to any obligations with you.

The Nonexistent Boyfriend is the man you will or will not hang out with on dates (your call, of course). He is the man you'll talk to on the phone, exchange text messages with, exchange photos with, and even have sex with. While all of these actions are blatant and appear as though a commitment should ensue, that may not be what your Nonexistent Boyfriend is thinking. He is definitely there in the flesh, but until he is on the same page with you emotionally and commits himself to only dating you, he is nonexistent. Simply put, the Nonexistent Boyfriend is not your man, your partner, significant other, spouse, mate, fiancé, better half, or companion. When you meet a man and begin to see him, he is *nonexistent*!

Throughout the course of this book, we'll refer to the Nonexistent Boyfriend as the NB. There's no deeper meaning behind the abbreviation other than me wanting to shorten the term now that you're aware of its meaning. In addition, I want to encourage you not to be dismayed while you date your NB. Your current or future NB might be exactly what you've been looking for in a partner, and that's good. If you meet a man who fits the bill, focus on what he's bringing to the table and enjoy the process of casually dating him. Don't make it one of your goals to get him to like you or be in a serious relationship with you sooner rather than later. He should be on an active quest to make you his woman, and if he's not, then he's not the one.

In many cases, your NB enters a friendship with you, taking it one day at a time. He doesn't see himself in a relationship with you yet because he's most likely trying to figure out what he wants from you. What he wants from you could be superficial (i.e., sex or a good time), or it could be worthwhile (i.e., a long-term commitment). If your NB decides he wants you for superficial reasons, it's not because you don't possess great qualities. Instead, it means your NB doesn't think he wants anything more than a friendship with you because you're not the one for him, and that's OK. Think of it this way: There are some cases in which *you* didn't want anything beyond a friendship with some of your past NBs. After learning more about them and spending some time with them, you realized they weren't the right match for you for whatever reason. Well, the same goes for your current or future NB; allow him to have those feelings, too.

Always take into account that you call the shots with your NB at *all* times. Knowing this means when you surrender your power and let any emotions get the best of you, you inadvertently let your NB call the shots and take what he wants from you. This isn't to say he has the right to take what he wants, but if you act on emotions rather than conscious decision making, your NB is liable to take you for granted.

Another element to consider while dating your NB is that he shouldn't be known to *everyone* in your circle without you being absolutely clear you're taking things to the next level with him. What this means is all your friends and family members shouldn't know everything about your NB. Refrain from letting your friends and family members know about every date you've gone on with him or every conversation you've shared with one another. Not sharing all the details about your NB early on is bigger than being private or tight-lipped. Refraining from sharing too many details early on puts your dating status with him at ease. Sharing too many details about your NB without knowing where you stand leads you to regard him as more than what he is. Constantly talking about your NB and painting a picture of him to others infiltrates your reality, and soon enough, you may inadvertently act out as someone who needs to live up to the picture you painted to everyone else.

Keep in mind that the likelihood of your NB mentioning details, or anything at all, about you to his friends is highly

## Who Is the Nonexistent Boyfriend (NB)?

unlikely. It's not that you're not beautiful, cool, or funny, it's just that your NB knows you're not his girlfriend, so he's not telling his friends or family members too many details as he's getting to learn and know more about you.

# Chapter Three

## WHO AM I TO THE NONEXISTENT BOYFRIEND (NB)?

Always consider that you're nonexistent in your NB's life, and he's nonexistent in yours until there's a commitment. You never want to regard your NB as more than what he is simply because you've concocted an elaborate idea in your mind of what you and your NB could possibly be in the future. In some cases, the NB puts on a façade. You may encounter an NB who verbally expresses his feelings toward you to create some sort of hope for you and him. It *is* possible that you may meet a man like this who is selfishly stringing you along. No matter his tactics, you have no control over what he chooses to do. You only have control over *your* actions and how you perceive him while you're casually dating him.

Again, don't be disappointed by this. The NB might not always be a negative part of your dating history. Like any friendship you set out to develop with a man, it has an outcome. Some friendships turn out successful and may develop into a commitment; some friendships may turn out regretful for several reasons, and some you won't even care enough about to create memories. No matter what the outcome is or what you predict the outcome to be, your NB is technically here to fulfill your physical and/or mental needs without a commitment. Should your feelings change and your emotions come into play, then make certain that your NB is just as emotionally satisfied and has the same positive, mutual feelings about being in a commitment with you.

Now that you're aware of what a Nonexistent Boyfriend (NB) is, it is also important to know you can have more than one at a time. Because you are not committed to *any* man you are casually dating, you are liable to date more than one NB if you choose to. Having more than one NB at a time forces you to refrain from becoming emotionally attached to anyone, which is a good move early on. Because the NB is not yours to claim and you are not his to claim, you are single until you decide otherwise. And because you have the option to casually date more than one NB at a time, your NB can do the same.

I want you to put what your NB experiences into perspective. As the NB, his viewpoint on things is naturally different than yours. Because he's a man, he's going to think and act like one. That means he'll use what power he has to date freely, openly, and carefree. He'll put himself in a position to be the bachelor he is and date women like you without having to be your partner. According to relationship psychologist Mairead Molloy, "Men are more prone to keeping their options open, potentially dating more than one person at once (in the early stages) and keeping an eye out for future options."[1] That said, your NB isn't taking into account who you are to him yet. When he's beginning to get to know you, he's dating you without restraints and expects you to date him that way, too.

You see, fully understanding who the NB is no matter how you feel, how he feels, what you say, or what he says will allow you to behave and date differently. You'll behave strategically and direct yourself in a way that won't have you emotionally investing more than you have to. It will allow

---

[1] Malread Molloy, *GQ Magazine*, "16 Ways Men and Women Date Differently, and First Date Tips for Both," Britain Edition, (June 2 2017) https://www.gq-magazine.co.uk/article/first-date-tips-for-men-and-women

you to date differently because you'll determine your status with him the same way he determines his status with you.

As you navigate through dating and considering potential NBs, allow every NB you casually date to be very up front with what he's looking for and what he believes he wants from dating in the very beginning. You want your next NB to be clear on what his immediate intentions are. Avoid asking your next NB how he feels about a future with you because he won't know that in the very beginning. Your NB should only be able to tell you what he's looking for from *any* woman in general and how he feels about committing to *any* woman, not just you. Beware, some NBs may sell you a dream with their words to get what they want out of you. The good news is you can usually pick up on these kinds of NBs and use your knowledge of who he is to dismiss him and move on. You'll also be aware of his deceitfulness because his actions will more than likely be his truth-teller rather than his words.

All in all, don't make the title of an NB greater than what it is. Don't mistake your current feelings for a NB with expectations you think should be met. Always take it a day at a time. If your NB is meant to be your boyfriend, it will happen with mutual feelings and a shared agreement. You won't have to beg or plead. It will happen effortlessly.

Below is a hypothetical scenario in which titles and roles

become blurred. Take note of how the woman in the scenario loses sight of where she stands with her NB and how it changes the dynamic of the friendship she established with him. Also, take note of how things could've turned out differently for her if she was more aware of her NB's role in her life.

## Scenario One
### KIM'S MISUNDERSTANDING

Kim went out one night with her girlfriends to a local bar for happy hour. This was nothing unusual for Kim, as she was embracing her newly single lifestyle. In the midst of sweaty dancing bodies, the clinking of wine glasses, and the yelling of nine-to-fivers, Kim was approached by Greg, a handsome professional who had no problem buying Kim and her friends a round of their favorite drinks. By the end of the night, Kim and Greg had talked about several different topics, such as their respective careers, their hobbies, their position on children, dating, and even sex. They eventually exchanged phone numbers and decided to speak to one another at a later time. Soon after, their phone conversations turned into weekly dates, and their dates eventually turned into late-night meetups here and there.

Phone calls with Greg consisted of laughter, recaps of comedy shows, and *vague* talks about men and women in dating. Besides Greg mentioning to Kim that he was single and dating other women when they first met, he never brought up relationships again. Kim never directly asked Greg about his dating status with other women because she didn't want to come across as "eager." On top of that, Kim and Greg had never really discussed being in a relationship with one another, even though some time had passed. Kim heard horror stories of people using the "r" word (relationship) before its time, so she stayed clear of going down that path unnecessarily.

On the backend, what Greg *didn't* know was that Kim had discovered him on different social media platforms long before they had gotten to know each other very well. Although Greg never mentioned he was active on social media platforms, Kim found him and would monitor his social interaction on different sites. Kim assumed Greg was not lying about being single because he never mentioned being in a relationship to her. He also never eluded to seeking interest in a particular woman on any of his social media platforms or in any of his photos online.

After four months of casually dating one another, Kim decided Greg would be her focus. At this stage, Kim hadn't been dating anyone else. She thought she didn't have to date other men because Greg was a "good catch," and she wanted to focus on one guy at a time so it wouldn't interfere with her search for Mr. Right. In addition to not wanting to date other men, Kim was content with the intimacy she had shared with Greg. Whenever they slept together, Greg referred to Kim as "baby" or "honey," which certainly heightened Kim's assumptions about Greg's feelings toward her. Kim's comfort in sleeping with one man was something she wanted to stick to moving forward.

What she liked most about Greg was that he threw compliments at her like a tennis ball in a Wimbledon match. To Greg, Kim was beautiful, sexy, funny, kind, sweet, and all the other adjectives that made a man want to lock a woman down. Kim *really* knew Greg liked her because, let's face it, his actions and terms of endearment said it all. Greg was not shy about wanting to take Kim out to dinner every once in a while or taking Kim out for ice cream every second Sunday after she got out of church. There was certainly a connection between them, so Kim thought, and she was here for it all.

Unexpectedly, phone calls decreased on Greg's end, dates became a chore, and compliments were only given when they were prompted with preceding questions. Kim became disappointed in Greg because of his change in behavior. Her expectations of him were very high, and this weird behavior wasn't like him—at least that's what Kim thought. To get answers, Kim asked Greg in one of their text conversations if he was still dating other people. It came out of nowhere because their text conversation wasn't on the topic of relationships. Greg abruptly responded, "No," and Kim went on to ask, "So why are you treating me like second place?"

Kim never received a reply from Greg. Days had passed,

and Kim felt defeated. At one point, things were going great. Now, it was as if Greg was a stranger. Hoping things would change and the tension would lessen, she reached out to Greg *again* with a simple "Hey." Once again, Kim never got a reply from Greg. As if these signs weren't enough, she reached out to him once more, this time with a lengthy text; Kim sent Greg to hell on a first-class flight.

Kim told Greg how much he had hurt her, and she even referred to him as a "dirty dog" because she was hurt. This was the second time a man she was casually dating did this to her. She felt betrayed, misled, and blindsided. In Kim's text, she went into detail about how Greg should've been honest with her and not led her to believe they were seriously dating when he knew he wanted something other than what it was. She also told him she stopped dating other men, and Greg selfishly made her believe that was OK. She laid out Greg's shortcomings and the fact that she dealt with them anyway, including how Greg wasn't that great in bed and that he came across as pretentious on social media. Kim also reminded Greg that she would delete his number from her phone and her memory; he was to never contact her again.

After Kim's extensive text message was delivered, she still never heard from Greg again. Although he disappeared from her life, Kim continued to follow his posts on social media and examine his whereabouts and activities.

## "Controlling Your Crazy" Solution

In Kim's situation with Greg, she didn't fully recognize who Greg was to her. He was indeed a friend, a great social companion, and he helped create a bond with her. However, if Kim had distinguished what she wanted out of dating versus what Greg wanted, her dating situation could've turned out differently. Kim was always in control of her actions. While she feared using the "r" word (relationship), Greg assumed there wouldn't be a relationship with Kim based on the mere fact that he never brought it up. Kim's reluctance to be honest and up front made Greg play it safe by rolling with the punches.

Kim should have had a discussion with Greg in their initial phone conversations regarding what he was looking for in dating her and other women. In those initial conversations, Kim wouldn't ask about Greg's intentions for her specifically because it would've been too early for him to make that decision; he didn't fully know her. However, Kim could've listened to what Greg had to say and decide then if they were on the same page as far as what they wanted out of dating other people.

If Kim decided to still hang out with Greg after his response, that would've been her prerogative and her judgement call. However, after four months of casually dating,

Kim had all the power to revisit any initial conversations about dating and relationships, making it about her the second time around. Based on Greg's response to Kim's questions or concerns, that is when Kim could've decided if she wanted to continue to invest her time and energy in Greg moving forward. If she decided to casually date him knowing he wasn't looking for a commitment, then Kim had to live with any outcome that resulted; Kim was, and still is, in control of her dating life. If Kim decided to casually date Greg because he led her to believe he was dating her with the purpose of seeing where things could go, then Kim couldn't be faulted for taking his word for it and assuming he had good intentions. However, in the example, Greg was vague with Kim, and she never revisited her position on dating or what Greg wanted out of their friendship. Greg took Kim out to dinner *occasionally*, he treated her to ice cream *sometimes*, and *never* engaged in conversations about dating Kim seriously.

Although Kim and Greg hit it off and seemed happy dating one another, there was no title between them; Kim wasn't Greg's girlfriend. Although Kim was owed the respect of having Greg explain his unusual behaviors, he more than likely used the fact that there were blurred lines between them to take advantage of the situation. For one, Kim could have had a serious conversation with Greg, either in person or over the phone. More than likely, Greg wouldn't be the one to initiate a conversation like this based on his actions (although he should), so if Kim wanted to exhibit the control she had over her actions, she had the power to arrange a mature conversation with him.

Remember, Kim was confused as to why Greg pulled away. To Kim, Greg pulling away didn't align with the man she spent some time with, who took her out on dates, had phone conversations with her, and enjoyed her company. Because Kim thought this way, she abruptly sent Greg an off-topic text as her way of getting an immediate answer while abandoning her emotional control. Greg's sudden fading behavior deserved attention. Although Greg's actions weren't the worst thing in the world, it is fair to say Kim was worthy of an explanation. How she went about getting it more than likely threw Greg for a loop, causing him to lie and be deceitful. Again, Greg used a lousy text conversation to his advantage to avoid what really needed to be a mature conversation.

Kim should've regarded Greg as her NB from day one. Until Greg asked Kim for a commitment, they were *not* a couple. Forcibly making Greg an NB would've put Kim in a position that didn't allow any confusion. She'd know that no matter what transpired (i.e., dates, sex), Greg was not in a committed relationship with her, especially if he didn't talk about it or if Kim didn't address it. Because Greg and Kim were progressing in their friendship without a title, Kim misunderstood where she stood in Greg's life.

Unfortunately, in the grand scheme of things, Greg's time with Kim was merely based on good sex, hot meals, phone calls, and weekend dates without any commitment over the course of four months. In Kim's mind, dating this way was good enough for her because Greg was showing he liked her the entire time, and she never wanted to throw Greg off by bringing up relationships or what his motives were; that was Kim's mistake. In fact, it was more of Greg's job to have had these conversations with Kim because, after all, he approached her when they met, he asked for her number, and he took her out while investing time and spending money.

It's important for Kim and every single woman to know that every man you casually date is and always will be your NB unless the situation evolves into a commitment. This does not take away from any time invested, money spent, or physical connections made; however, establishing what role you play and what role your NB plays will make lines clear very early on while eliminating the possibility of confusion later. Never be intimidated by the questions you think need to be answered. Sure, asking questions that involve relationships and dating can seem nerve-racking, but if you want to date without the fear of uncertainty, you need your important questions answered.

Asking your NB questions shouldn't feel like a kill-drill session in which the two of you are making each other uneasy. However, upon meeting him and engaging in conversations, simple questions, like "Are you currently dating someone seriously?" "Are you looking for a commitment with someone while you're on the dating scene?" and "Are you ready for a serious relationship if you meet the right person?" are perfectly harmless. Your NB should be asking you similar questions as well. If he's *only* interested in questions that revolve around your hobbies, your preferences in food, your career, and/or your social lifestyle, you should make sure you're having him answer the questions you think are important to *you*.

## Chapter Four

## CONTROLLING YOUR CRAZY WHILE DATING YOUR NONEXISTENT BOYFRIEND

Controlling your crazy while dating your Nonexistent Boyfriend is not as difficult as you may think it is; however, it *is* something that must be deliberately practiced like any other behavioral technique. You now know what it means to control your crazy, and you're well-aware of who your Nonexistent Boyfriend is, so together, controlling your crazy while dating your Nonexistent Boyfriend means controlling the urge to release irrational or unreasonable emotions while dating a man who's not *your* man.

To go into it further, controlling your crazy while dating your Nonexistent Boyfriend is about holding back all the irresponsible things you want to say to your NB because it would have no bearing on your dating situation. Irresponsible things usually refer to putting your NB down, poking fun at him, or cursing him out because he did something you did not like or didn't expect him to do. Instead of maturely addressing the situation you're upset about, leaning on insults and mocking your NB is the irresponsible way out. When you restrain from these sorts of behaviors, it shows you're able to control your crazy while dating him.

Controlling your crazy while dating your Nonexistent Boyfriend is also about holding out on physical actions you want to commit because it wouldn't make the outcome with your NB change. Physical actions can include hitting your NB, damaging his personal belongings, rummaging through his home/car, hacking his computer/phone device, constantly following his activity on social media sites, or driving by his house unannounced. Again, when you focus on what is really bothering you or what you find concerning, you're controlling your emotions in a way that could have your questions or concerns addressed. However, taking matters into your own hands by lurking around, sneaking where you don't belong, or damaging things is a sure sign your "crazy" needs to be transformed into a more tactful approach.

I can't stress enough that controlling your crazy doesn't mean you don't say how you feel or mute your emotions toward *any* NB you date. It means you choose the *right* words and the *appropriate* emotions for the situation you're in. Your job is to control emotions that may not be warranted, but if they are, it's OK to project them in a way that is clear and makes sense for the situation you're in.

In other words, using emotional intelligence is controlling your crazy. For instance, if you are casually dating a man for six months and you think it's time for you to meet his mother, there's a way you should go about addressing that. First, consider that he hasn't asked you to be serious with him yet (because if he did, you'd be in a relationship). Also consider that he hasn't scheduled a meetup with you and his mother (because if he did, this wouldn't be a concern for you). Knowing this, you'd now have to ask yourself, *Why is it important for me to meet his mother? Is it important to him that I meet his mother? Is he waiting for us to be in a relationship before I meet his mother?* And when you reflect by asking these sorts of questions, you can have a conversation with your NB that is appropriate for your current dating situation.

For a woman in a situation like this, addressing where she and her NB stand is of utmost importance. Once that is addressed, asking about the meetup with his mother would make more sense. If a woman is casually dating an NB who tells her he's not sure what he wants or isn't thinking about a relationship with her, then bringing up a meeting with his mother would be pointless. Keep in mind, an NB who doesn't bring up important things, like relationship statuses and meeting family members, will think you're jumping the gun when you're really not (in some cases). Therefore, it is best to evaluate your dating situation with your NB and use emotional intelligence to speak about how you feel.

Many times, having to control your crazy while dating your Nonexistent Boyfriend occurs when the outcome you hoped for doesn't play out. One instance could be your involvement with an NB who doesn't define where you and he stand. Another instance could be an NB who led you to believe there'd be more from the friendship and, for whatever reason, he pulled away from you. Let's be frank, your NB will enter a friendship with you thinking of you as a blank slate. He knows *nothing* substantial about you (usually), and in most cases, he's going at your pace while keeping his intentions in the

> *I can't stress enough that controlling your crazy doesn't mean you don't say how you feel or mute your emotions toward any NB you date. It means you choose the right words and the appropriate emotions for the situation you're in. Your job is to control emotions that may not be warranted, but if they are, it's OK to project them in a way that is clear and makes sense for the situation you're in.*

background. Knowing this, you have the power to dictate everything you say and do. Once you're aware of this power, your chances of going crazy are slim, and controlling your crazy while dating your Nonexistent Boyfriend becomes second nature.

Controlling your crazy while dating your Nonexistent Boyfriend also means withholding the first words or actions that come to mind when they're feeling emotional. Many women tend to react in the now instead of taking in what has occurred and strategically calculating how they'll react toward their NB. As a result of not reflecting momentarily, I'm constantly asked the same questions from single women, who, at some point, have gone crazy: "How do I resist not saying how I feel the moment I find out he lies to me? What if my back is against the wall, and I have to say something so I can move on? What if he does something to upset me? My response for every woman with these questions or similar ones is the same: Evaluate all the signs your NB shows you, both good and bad. Did the good signs progress into even greater actions, or were they stagnant? How early did you notice the bad signs? Were these bad signs accompanied by lies? Did you ever address these bad signs? And if you did, did you do anything about it?

When you reflect in this way, you'll be able to carefully consider your next move with your NB. It will also lead to questions you should answer regarding your own actions, like, *Was I OK with casually dating my NB knowing he told me substantial lies? Was I OK sleeping with my NB without a commitment?* or *Was I fine casually dating my NB although I knew I was receiving subpar treatment from him?* Answering questions like these puts you in the mindset to be someone who is accountable and in control of her actions.

Your NB doesn't, and will never, have the final say when it comes to what *you* want to do. Whether he's asking you out on a date, asking you to come over to his place, asking for sex, or asking you to be in a serious relationship with him, you have the final say and all the control. That said, controlling your crazy while dating your Nonexistent Boyfriend falls on the way you react.

Considering all these things makes it easy and comfortable for you to control your crazy while dating your Nonexistent Boyfriend. Controlling your crazy allows you to do a lot of self-reflecting, and it gives you permission to take responsibility for your actions moving forward with your NB. Controlling your crazy while dating your Nonexistent Boyfriend forces you to take a step back and consider what may have ended the friendship between you two or what may have momentarily put a damper on things. Controlling your crazy means recognizing red flags and not letting them pile up until you lash out later; it means saying how you feel about something instead of mouthing off because you think he needs to be reprimanded. Controlling your crazy is about recognizing your value, walking away from what doesn't serve you, and not weakening your standards because a man you're casually dating broke a date or didn't call you for a few days. Controlling your crazy is trading in his unlikeable behavior for your sanity. No woman (that means you) should be overwhelmed or stressed about something as simple as dating. If your NB doesn't know how to date you or doesn't want to date you seriously, then there's no point in sticking around just to go crazy later. Always remember your instant ability to be in control.

## Chapter Five

## DITCHING OLD HABITS SO YOU CAN CONTROL YOUR CRAZY INDEFINITELY

Now, let's discuss very subtle acts that might occur while you are dating your NB. These are the acts that tend to get overlooked because you don't think they're worth being looked at. These acts aren't overt but are still considered "crazy" because it can rob you of your emotional peace.

To emphasize once more, "crazy" isn't always about yelling, cursing, fighting, acting belligerent, having a fit, or getting physical. "Crazy" is also thinking in a way that isn't healthy or beneficial toward your friendship with your NB. It's engaging in negative thinking or destructive subtle acts that can cause you to go overboard in your thought process.

This kind of crazy interrupts the natural dating process for you and your NB.

For example, some single women, because of past hurt or experiences, attempt to find information on their NB by creeping around as a form of a "got ya!" tactic. Past hurts aren't good feelings, and past experiences are what shape us and make us better daters. However, plotting against or sneakily trying to unveil secrets about an NB is the surest way to go crazy when you don't have to.

Searching your NB's social media page for clues that could lead you to "catch him" in an act is one example. That would involve you always looking at the activity on his social media page(s), reading the comments other people leave on his page(s) in an attempt to piece clues together, or date-matching photos to times you were or weren't with him. Another subtle crazy act could be searching for your NB's ex-girlfriend on social media networks or googling his ex for subliminal clues. Like with his page, you lurk on his ex's social media page(s) to try and figure out her social activity and piece together your own clues so you can question your NB later down the line. Does every single woman engage in these kinds of acts? Of course, not. However, if you find yourself ever going there, you've unnecessarily slipped into acting crazy.

I remember a former co-worker of mine who shared

with me her desire to know more about the NB she had met, had a few phone conversations with (way before the days of constant texting), and had gone out with a couple of times. I encouraged her to openly date her NB and see what it could lead to. On the backend, however, she frequently told me about her NB's late-night work hours, his extensive lunch breaks, and the overtime he put in at his job. All of it made her suspicious. As a result, she would drive to see if he was where he really said he was at lunch, and she would secretly call his job pretending to be someone else to see if he was really there. I couldn't understand why she was convincing herself that creepily checking on him was the way to go. I encouraged my former co-worker to let things play out with her newfound NB and to not interrupt the natural flow of things. I also let her know she was in control. If she didn't like how many hours her NB spent at work or if it made her uncomfortable to date someone with an intense schedule like his, she had the option of dating other men *or* choosing not to casually date her NB any longer. She had all the power in the world to let him know she was looking for something other than what he brought to the table. Let's just say my former co-worker and her former NB didn't work out. Her crazy antics caught up with her, and her former NB was not here for *any* of it.

The examples and actions I described may not be obvious

to you because you might be accustomed to behaving this way based on your actions or the actions of other women you know. However, these actions can cause *any* woman to lose her cool or react prematurely, all for the sake of being ahead of the game instead of holding on to the control she already had. Imagine meeting a good guy who likes you and wants to know more about you, but all that gets ruined because of unnecessary probing and assumptions on your end. No man is perfect; trust me. I know this because no human is perfect. Nevertheless, that imperfect man can be perfect for you if you let your casual dating play out and rid yourself of the crazy acts that could get you emotionally stirred.

And I get it. No woman wants to feel slighted or be caught off guard while she's dating her NB. But putting yourself in a vulnerable position for no reason and avoiding asking questions by doing your own sneaky investigations will cause you to react in a crazy way when your NB does something you don't agree with or says something that rubs you the wrong way.

Controlling your crazy while dating your Nonexistent Boyfriend should look like two things: 1) using emotional intelligence to remain subdued in your approach toward your NB, and 2) being honest and up front at all times with your NB.

Some NBs are known for doing some shitty things,

some are actually quality men who just didn't work out for you, and some turn out to be your partners for a period of time or even a lifetime. No matter what their position ends up being, you *must* evaluate every situation you're up against and approach it with rationality and emotional stability. Controlling your crazy while dating your Nonexistent Boyfriend is an honest approach that allows you to control the emotions that want to leap out and avoid opening yourself up to extreme vulnerability or scrutiny.

As a takeaway, controlling your crazy while dating your Nonexistent Boyfriend isn't about being someone you're not, and it's not about covering things up so you can only see the bright side of things. It's about setting the record straight with your NB without becoming wrapped up in activities that cause you to be on edge or uncertain about your power. When you control your crazy, you confront every situation by speaking up (not crying or whining), you confirm your dating status with him (without demanding it or giving ultimatums/threats), and you stand firm in your actions (without being led by rash emotions or falsities you've conjured up in your mind).

Below is an example of a fictitious NB who engaged in behaviors that made the woman he was casually dating upset. Take note of how the woman was able to control her crazy while dating her NB.

## Scenario 2
### LEXI CALLS IT QUITS

Lexi had been single for the last five years, meaning she hadn't been in a relationship with a man she could call her *boyfriend*. It's not that Lexi didn't want a boyfriend, but she couldn't control what life had dealt her when it came to dating. What Lexi *never* wanted was to commit to a man for the sake of having a boyfriend. She wanted something real and genuine; she wanted a boyfriend who brought her complete happiness.

Lexi, at one time in her life, was even eager to get married; the idea of marriage used to make Lexi smile. She always looked forward to walking down the aisle, and her idea of sharing her world with a man she loved for the rest of her life was a dream to her. While marriage was important for Lexi, she gave up on the idea of it to focus on landing a boyfriend first.

At this point, Lexi was comfortable with being single; she separated her wants from her reality and embraced the process of the right man finding her as she explored her options. However, it was weird for her. Although she was comfortable with *tables for one* and dinners on the couch alone, she was also mentally exhausted from her dating experiences. What exhausted Lexi the most was that none of her dates would ever stick or progress into anything greater after a certain point. It was like her dating life had a two-month curse she couldn't break. Her dating escapades would all have similar beginnings and endings, and she was fed up with trying to figure out why men couldn't seem to get on the same page as her while they attempted to develop their friendship.

In the beginning of most of Lexi's experiences with a new NB, she would be optimistic and excited for another chance at getting to know someone new. For the most part, the NBs Lexi met appeared to like her after meeting her and learning about her on the surface. Initial phone conversations would always graduate to a few dates, and dates would soon evolve into intimacy. Unfortunately, it seemed like after a month or two, Lexi's NBs would pull away, and Lexi would go back to square one. At the age of forty, Lexi was convinced the NBs she was meeting and going out with were all the same; they were *inconsistent*. Despite their inconsistency, Lexi never passed on the chance to meet someone special and start from scratch.

That said, Lexi was up for another dating adventure. In one of Lexi's many visits to the gym, she met a trainer named Lee. Lee was smart, attractive, in shape, and was someone Lexi always saw around but never spoke to because he wasn't "her type." Although he had some physical traits that appealed to her, he appeared arrogant, and *that* was a turnoff for her. However, when Lee approached Lexi during one of her gym visits, he was a charmer. He was the exact opposite of what Lexi imagined, and he even invited Lexi to a free training session with him. Lee was charismatic, kind, and well-spoken, and that made Lexi give in to his request.

For the next two months, Lexi and Lee casually dated and hit it off. Their personalities meshed, they enjoyed similar outings, and for the first time in a long time, Lexi didn't feel mentally beaten down by her past experiences. Not a weekend went by without Lexi seeing Lee, and there wasn't a night he didn't put her to sleep during one of their extended phone conversations. At this point, Lexi's gym visits were way more appealing than before, and she even stepped out on a limb by telling her friends about the man she was spending time with.

Lexi was aware that Lee was only her NB, and she was fine with that. For one, it was too early for her to decide if he would be her boyfriend, and she and Lee established early on what they were in search of and agreed that, together, they would date one day at a time and see where things went. They were both in search of a relationship with the right person, and they both made it clear that neither of them would rush into anything prematurely.

Besides things going smoothly between Lexi and Lee, he also never gave Lexi a reason not to trust him, and that's what she liked the most. In the short time they had known each other, Lee seemed very up front and honest with Lexi and never raised suspicions that would otherwise make her give in to her doubts. His answers to Lexi's questions always felt complete, and he prided himself on "telling it like it is."

One question, which Lee initiated, struck Lexi in a peculiar way. Usually, she'd be the one asking her NB if he was still dating other people after casually dating for some time, but this time around, Lee wanted first dibs at knowing who Lexi was seeing. Lee asked Lexi about her dating status with other men and convinced her that his curiosity was based on the fact that he decided not to date other women anymore. He shared with Lexi that he liked her and wanted to focus on dating one woman. Lexi agreed to the voice in her head and gave Lee a huge "OK!" Lexi was finally dating someone who wanted to progress into something greater than an NB. Although Lee had not asked Lexi to be in a relationship with him, he convinced her that she would be at the center of his attention.

On one particular evening, Lexi went out with her friends to dinner. They laughed, drank, reminisced on old jokes, and embraced the hours they were spending with each other. To Lexi's surprise, Lee walked into the same restaurant hand-in-hand with another woman. The embrace the other woman gave Lee made Lexi's stomach sink. It was an embrace Lexi knew all too well because she was guilty of giving Lee the same affectionate smile and gaze this woman had.

Lee was unaware of Lexi's presence in the restaurant. He was completely oblivious to Lexi's bird's eye view of his table with another woman. Lexi and her friends watched as Lee and another woman shared their first round of drinks and kissed while they waited to put in their food orders. Lexi's friends put in their fair share of peer pressure, convincing her to confront Lee while he embarrassed her and dined with someone else. Lexi thought about throwing drinks in his face, and she thought about walking up to the other woman and giving her a heads up about Lee's conniving behavior, but she did the opposite.

She paid her bill, got up, and left without ever letting Lee know what she saw. Lexi's fifteen-minute drive home felt like an hour-long drive because she felt like Lee got the best of her. He wasn't her boyfriend, but Lexi thought she was on her way to becoming Lee's girlfriend based on their most recent conversation about not seeing other people. Lexi thought to herself, *Lee was the one who wanted to know my status. Lee was the one who called me every night and took me out frequently. Lee was the one who approached me at the gym and asked for my number.* Lexi pondered on everything that transpired over the last two months with Lee and thought she had done everything the "right way." It was Lee who messed up.

The following day, Lexi called Lee over the phone. She told him what she saw the night before and how she felt about it. When Lee tried to interrupt her thoughts, she asked for the floor without being disrespected or interrupted. Lee gave her the floor for about ten minutes, and it felt *good* for Lexi to express her feelings while also letting him know he ruined a cool friendship between them.

Lexi let Lee know that she trusted the things he told her and trusted that he meant well for their friendship. She also let him know that she never had a problem with him seeing other women; her problem was that he lied about it to create another narrative for himself, and that was unfair. Lexi ended her phone conversation with Lee by telling him to respectfully lose her number. She assured him that he shouldn't call or text her again because it was likely she wouldn't respond. Although Lexi wanted to curse him out and get some satisfaction out of four-letter words and insults, she knew that wouldn't change the fact that Lee had already planned a date with another woman, took her out, and lied about his intentions.

Lexi controlled the sappy emotions that wanted to leap out *so* badly and decided to express herself in a way that would let Lee know that, although they weren't a couple, what he did was still deceitful. Unfortunately, Lexi's two-month curse hadn't been broken, but she felt okay knowing that if she met a new man and felt comfortable and confident around him, he deserved a fair chance at casually dating her if he asked for it.

You see, Lee liked Lexi. It was obvious based on the things he said and did. Only Lee knows why he was out with another woman when he stated Lexi would be his focus. Did Lexi make a bad move, giving Lee the okay to date him exclusively? Not really. Lexi followed what felt right to her, and that's okay too. However, when Lee told Lexi about his desire to only date her, he should've also defined their status. Did Lee's willingness to focus only on Lexi mean they were a couple? Did Lee asking Lexi to not date other men mean no one else could claim her because Lee was claiming her as his

> girlfriend? Those are the defining questions, and that is where Lee should've stepped up. Because he didn't, Lexi should've defined her position with Lee by asking him what he wanted out of dating exclusively, so she'd be sure on his thinking, as well as hers.
>
> Unfortunately, Lee ended up misleading Lexi, and it was no longer Lexi's job to figure out where Lee's head was after seeing him out with someone else. Lexi stated her piece with Lee, voiced her feelings, and made a clear exit from a man who was headed down the wrong path with her.

Controlling your crazy while dating your Nonexistent Boyfriend can be difficult in certain situations, but stopping, reflecting, and giving yourself a moment to gather your emotions will set the tone for any and every NB you encounter. While some instances don't require hours or a full day of reflection, you can still put a halt on leading with the first words or actions that come to mind when you're upset or bothered by something your NB did.

In a lot of cases, your NB will convince himself that your actions aren't called for when he does something negative, and he'll blame everything on you responding in an emotional or "crazy" way. He does this self-convincing because he'll rely on the fact that the two of you aren't in a commitment with one another or that you really are acting crazy. On the other hand, there are a lot of NBs who won't call you crazy but, instead, will submit to your decision to walk away or no longer date them. This only happens when your response to who you think he is and what he's done (or hasn't done) are directly aligned with his wrongdoings. Your NB will know that, although the two of you aren't in a commitment together, what he did was possibly hurtful, confusing, or just not on the same page as you, and he will no longer have a brewing friendship with you.

Take a moment to reflect on any past experiences you've had with an NB. In any of those experiences, were you unable to control your crazy? In addition, reflect on other experiences where you may have subtly engaged in "crazy" actions as a way to dig into your NB's past or secretly gain knowledge about him. In any of your subtle crazy actions, did you find it difficult to control your emotions because you were overthinking or making rash assumptions toward your NB? It's also important to reflect on past experiences you've had with an NB and decide if you *were* able to control your crazy while dating him. How did it feel? Did you get what you wanted out of it? Did you walk away knowing you still had control and power over your actions and the things you said?

# Chapter Six

## HOW TO CONTROL YOUR CRAZY AFTER A HURT PAST

If you've endured at least one breakup or a hurtful relationship in your lifetime, then you have a past that's worth acknowledging. For many single women, that past could be one full of regrets and unfortunate turmoil. For other single women, that past could consist of many life-long lessons and friendships with exes. Whatever the outcome of your past, you have one and you can't ignore whatever caused you and your ex to split. Whether the split was your fault or the fault of your ex, acknowledging that the breakup occurred and using the relationship to reform old habits, is what this chapter is about. It's a way to reflect on your past, while using it to push forward so you can build healthy relationships with the men you date.

If *any* of your past relationships involved physical, emotional, or verbal abuse, I'm sure you want to rid yourself of the negative scenarios that occurred within the relationship. More than likely, you'd also want to dismiss the memory of the times you wanted out but decided to stay anyway. However, don't be so quick to dismiss these past relationships. Your experience is the tool you'll need to shape your new dating life and create healthy ways to interact with the men you'll meet. It is important to note that the hurt from our old relationships shouldn't manipulate how you respond to the new men you encounter. If it *does* occur, and it tremendously affects the friendships you try to build with NBs, then counseling would have to take place so you can fully heal before moving on to something fresh.

For relationships you were in that didn't endure abuse, but crumbled because of non-abusive mishaps here and there, there's still a space that could potentially have you wanting to control your crazy. This is not to say there's no hope for avoiding going crazy after a relationship, rather, not making intentional decisions regarding your emotions after a breakup could have you consumed with old thoughts and tired habits.

\*\*\*

Because you've had past dating experiences, you'll enter new friendships with men and you'll bring your memories from the past along with you; this is completely normal if you're a human being. Memories provide us with experiences that can turn into lessons. These lessons guide us into making better choices about men, they allow us to work through any imperfections we might possess, and they prepare us for what's out there in the dating world.

Bringing your memories with you into new friendships with men only becomes an issue when they negatively affect your reactions to behaviors from your NB. While your memories *do* shape your present and future, negative parts of your past relationships shouldn't have an effect on how you behave with new men you want to date.

> **While your memories do shape your present and future, negative parts of your past relationships shouldn't have an effect on how you behave with new men you want to date.**

The inability to control your behavior and emotions (stemming from the past) can result in never creating solid relationships or it can have you feeling trapped by what someone else did to hurt you or upset you.

For example, my experience with Jason consisted of a lot of lies. There were lies told to me when we were in a relationship together and there were lies told to me after the relationship ended and he became my NB. There were good memories I took with me after we broke up, and there were the ones that led to my crazy college experience. Despite any negative feelings or negative memories I took away from my relationship with Jason, I knew I had to detach myself from those feelings if I wanted to develop new memories with new people. Learning how to control my crazy after my breakup with Jason was not easy, but it was important. There were times I was on edge because I thought all men were liars and cheaters; I thought this way because of my past experience. However, I let go of those thoughts because I knew all men were different, and I knew I never wanted to go down the same road I had traveled when I was dating Jason.

I got to this place by acknowledging that my past happened, accepting all that occurred in the relationship, and embracing the opportunity to start over. I also knew if I didn't want to rehash negative feelings I had for Jason or revisit bad experiences I went through with him, then I had to focus on what made me happy while I dated new people, without the interference of stale feelings for someone else.

Your NB will have his fair share of memories and a past also; he is not exempt from the feelings that you have. However, he is responsible for dealing with his own past as you are yours. He should avoid using his past to control his fate with you and you should follow suit. Controlling your crazy after a hurt past doesn't mean you move on and forget everything that has happened to you. It means you don't engage in actions that would have you accusing your NB of things he didn't do, assuming he feels a particular way when he doesn't or imposing your life onto his because of your old experiences. Doing this can have your past get in the way of establishing great friendships and possibly potential relationships with the men you'll casually date. Just because an ex or former NB did something that crushed you, every man after him shouldn't get the brunt of the bad behavior you endured.

Use your knowledge of what controlling your crazy is and prevent yourself from projecting old thoughts onto new men. Your goal is to be the best version of yourself while dating your NB, and the last thing you want to do is have him meet the old you, stemming from a dead relationship. Here are some ways you can control the emotions from your past so it won't affect the friendship you're building with your NB:

- Consider him a new person when you meet him. He is not the same person as your ex or former NB.
- Listen to what he says as his truth. Until you can prove him otherwise or until you know he's a liar, take what he says as the truth.

- Make him aware of the decisions and boundaries you've created for yourself in order to feel safe emotionally
- Let your NB be exactly who he is without you projecting your personality on him.
- Understand that he is not perfect.
- Understand that you are not perfect.
- Remember that he has a past just as much as you do; if he's willing to work past his experiences, you should too.
- If you're known to react quickly when you're angry, and that didn't work in the past, make an effort to change that habit.
- Refrain from mentioning your ex or former NB in conversations that aren't aligned to what you're discussing.
- Refrain from discussing his ex and bringing his past into conversations that aren't aligned to what you're discussing.

Again, if you are not restored after a relationship or experience that has left you broken, then you'll need assistance with healing; professional help would yield the best result. On the other hand, if you've gone through relationships that expired due to reasons that may not have necessarily required professional help, then leaving your past ways behind you and becoming optimistic about what your new NB can bring to the table is something to look forward to.

All in all, you know what "crazy" is at this point, and you should be fully aware of who the NB is. With these newfound terms, I challenge you to casually date men with a different perspective. Use the next chapter to gauge your emotions and jot down your old way of thinking compared to what you know now. Try your hardest to reflect on your experiences by pulling out true events so you can get the most out of the exercise.

# Chapter Five

## CONTROLLING YOUR CRAZY

### DIY (Do It Yourself) Scenarios

## Scenario 1:

Your current Nonexistent Boyfriend tells you he no longer wants to continue going on dates with you. He feels overwhelmed by life's stressors, and he prefers to call the friendship quits; he's ready to go his separate way. At this point, you have already slept with your Nonexistent Boyfriend and have introduced him to all of your friends. You thought he was a potential boyfriend after three months of date nights and plenty of intimacy.

**Can you relate to this scenario?** _____

**If so, what happened?**
_____
_____

**Write down one to three things you did as a result of this scenario.**
_____
_____

**What was the outcome?**
_____
_____

**Considering that you now know how to control your crazy, what would you have done differently?**
_____
_____

## Scenario 2:

You discover that your Nonexistent Boyfriend's ex-girlfriend is on the same social media platform as you. Your inquiring mind wants to see what's on her personal social media page, but her personal page is set to "private." To see her page, you must request a connection.

Can you relate to this scenario? _____

If so, what happened?
_____
_____

Write down one to three things you did as a result of this scenario.
_____
_____

What was the outcome?
_____
_____

Considering that you now know how to control your crazy, what would you have done differently?
_____
_____

## Scenario 3:

After two consistent weeks of your Nonexistent Boyfriend acting "weird" and not calling you like he used to, you become suspicious. You know something isn't right, but you can't put your finger on it. You see him being active on different social media sites, so you know nothing's wrong with him.

**Can you relate to this scenario?** _____

**If so, what happened?**
_____
_____

**Write down one to three things you did as a result of this scenario.**
_____
_____

**What was the outcome?**
_____
_____

**Considering that you now know how to control your crazy, what would you have done differently?**
_____
_____

## Scenario 4:

You've been in an on-again-off-again relationship with your Nonexistent Boyfriend for the last eight months. When you're fed up with your NB's inconsistent antics and inability to court you properly, you cut ties and sever the friendship with him. When he realizes he's messed up, he always convinces you to rekindle the friendship, and you oblige every time. This last time around, you accepted your NB's invitation to begin casually dating again, but he drops a bomb on you by saying he no longer has interest in a committed relationship in the future.

**Can you relate to this scenario?** _____

**If so, what happened?**
_____
_____

**Write down one to three things you did as a result of this scenario.**
_____
_____

**What was the outcome?**
_____
_____

**Considering that you now know how to control your crazy, what would you have done differently?**
_____
_____

## Scenario 5:

Upon meeting your Nonexistent Boyfriend, he tells you he's dating other women; it doesn't bother you. However, after five months of going out on dates with him, meeting his friends, and even going on vacation with him, he's let you know that he's still seeing other women and is not sure if he's ready for a commitment with *any* woman. Your NB assumed you'd be fine with him seeing other women because you never objected to it initially and you never brought it up in conversation again. *You* assumed he had stopped seeing other women because you and him were progressing in friendship, seeing each other frequently and acting as a couple, although you weren't.

**Can you relate to this scenario?** _____

**If so, what happened?**

_____
_____

**Write down one to three things you did as a result of this scenario.**

_____
_____

**What was the outcome?**

_____
_____

**Considering that you now know how to control your crazy, what would you have done differently?**

_____
_____

# CYCQs FOR DATING

## (Controlling Your Crazy Quotes: A Recap of References to Remember While Dating)

**"First and foremost, a single woman is *not* to blame for having feelings and wanting to honor what a man tells her. She should not be made to feel guilty for feeling."**

You're allowed to feel and shouldn't be remorseful about it. If a man you're dating hurts your feelings, acknowledge it by admitting what he did and addressing it with him if that makes you more comfortable to move forward.

**"The reality of dating today is that women *always* have control with the men they meet."**

Never forget this principle. From the start of any conversation or date, you're in the driver's seat. You only give up your control when you believe you never had it to begin with.

**"I can't stress enough that controlling your crazy doesn't mean you don't say how you feel, or you mute your emotions toward *any* Nonexistent Boyfriend you date. It means you choose the *right* words and the *appropriate* emotions for the situation you're in."**

Remember to always express yourself, but let your words match your situation. If he didn't call you back when he was supposed to, your response to that shouldn't involve rage, tears, or extreme frustration. Or if he's struggling with taking you out on dates, you should avoid forcing him to step up and instead, move on without a fight because you know you deserve better. Express yourself in a way that is controlled and aligns with what happened to you rather than what you *wanted* to happen if things went perfectly.

**"This Nonexistent Boyfriend is the man who is physically attainable but serves no purpose emotionally because he hasn't committed to a relationship with you nor has he promised himself to any obligations with you."**

Again, be truthful about his position in your life. It's OK to call him "friend" or refer to him as "the guy you're hanging out with," but don't elevate his title to what you want it to be. Until he commits, he's nonexistent.

**"A man should not be emotionally obligated to a woman he's not committed to, and the same goes for a woman who's not committed to a man; no man should hold her to an emotional standard."**

As much as you shouldn't make the man you're casually dating abide by your rules on how to like you or date you, he shouldn't make you abide by any of his emotional rules, either. You're getting to know each other so it can build into something greater; there should be no pressure for titles, emotional connections, or made-up rules.

**"Because you shouldn't enter into a commitment with *any* man while casually dating, you are liable to casually date more than one Nonexistent Boyfriend if you choose to."**

This CYCQ is great to always take with you because you should not be afraid or ashamed to date more than one man at a time. For you to get to know men and have options, you have to date them, and sometimes that might mean simultaneously.

**"Women are in charge of what information they give *and* what information they take away from men the moment they meet them."**

Never blame your Nonexistent Boyfriend for what he knows about you. Any factor about your personal life that is shared is because you wanted it to be shared. If you're not ready to share personal things about yourself, don't share it; it's always your call. Whatever information your Nonexistent Boyfriend shares with you is yours to keep, digest, and process. You're in charge of what you do with his information also.

**"No woman wants to feel slighted or be caught off guard while she's casually dating her Nonexistent Boyfriend."**

Always remember to ask your Nonexistent Boyfriend the questions you think are important and appropriate to the conversation you're having. One way to avoid being caught off guard or feeling like the sheet got pulled over your eyes is to ask questions and get answers. This doesn't mean you pester him and go crazy; it means you ask questions to get to know him and connect the dots as you move along while casually dating him.

> **"Controlling your crazy while dating your Nonexistent Boyfriend should look like two things: 1) using emotional intelligence to remain subdued in your approach toward your Nonexistent Boyfriend, and 2) being honest and up front at all times with your Nonexistent Boyfriend."**

Use the emotional intelligence you're equipped with. When you move in an emotionally intelligent way, you can avoid off-track thinking. You'll approach every situation, both positive and negative, with rationale, and you'll more than likely be calm in your attitude. You never want to come across confused or sappy when speaking to him about something important, so this is major. Also remember to always be honest. If his questions toward you are not out of line or insulting, answer them honestly. Your honesty is a sure way to ensure he'll be honest with you, too. Take this mantra with you on every single date or encounter with your Nonexistent Boyfriend.

> **"Whether a man *thinks* he has reasons for referring to you as "crazy" is up to him; you're not bound by his title."**

Sometimes a man (usually immature and bad-mannered) may call you "crazy" when you're not. If your current or future Nonexistent Boyfriend refers to you as such, know you're not bound to his title. Stand firm on what you know to be true and how you feel. If he calls you crazy for no apparent reason other than you wanting the truth out of a situation, then *he's* the crazy one. State what you feel and move on to someone else who won't go down this route of calling you crazy. You want a Nonexistent Boyfriend who can address where either of you went wrong, even if it means calling the friendship quits.

**"Controlling your crazy doesn't mean you're not allowed to cry, express sappy emotions, mope, whine, or yell. Instead, it means you should *never* cry, express sappy emotions, mope, whine, or yell to/at the man you're casually dating for *any* reason if you can help it."**

This one is huge. Your Nonexistent Boyfriend will find it hard to hear you through tears, yelling, whining, or any other distracting sound. When your emotions are under control and your thoughts are processed, speak to your Nonexistent Boyfriend about whatever pertains to you and him. You never want to be so overly emotional that he blocks out your message and takes your vulnerability as a sign of weakness. Most importantly, you don't want the expression of your emotions to be viewed as unimportant if he thinks it's the method you use to get your points across.

**"Putting yourself in a vulnerable position for no reason and avoiding asking questions by doing your own sneaky investigations will cause you to react in a crazy way when your Nonexistent Boyfriend does something you don't agree with or says something that rubs you the wrong way."**

Point blank, avoid sneaking around for answers. Let this CYCQ resonate. The quickest way to go crazy is to investigate his life outside of what he shares with you. Going on the hunt for answers to questions you've mustered up is a sign that your emotions are hard to manage. Your reaction to his every move is bound to be off the wall, and it will show in how you respond to him. Leave his social media pages alone, avoid searching his personal belongings, and don't spy on him. If you let your friendship with your Nonexistent Boyfriend play out naturally, your response to his behaviors will, too. They won't be predicated on what you think you know or what you think you've discovered.

Thank you for reading
*Controlling Your Crazy While Dating Your Nonexistent Boyfriend*
If you enjoyed this book or found it helpful, please help spread the word with an online review.

## KEEP IN TOUCH WITH TONI DOUGLAS

Website: www.controllingyourcrazy.com
Facebook: Controlling Your Crazy
Instagram: @controllingyourcrazy

www.ingramcontent.com/pod-product-compliance
Lightning Source LLC
Chambersburg PA
CBHW021411290426
44108CB00010B/485